Rainbow
A SPECTRUM OF POEMS

DEEPIKA ARORA

BLUEROSE PUBLISHERS
India | U.K.

Copyright © Deepika Arora 2024

All rights reserved by author. No part of this publication may be reproduced, stored in a retrieval system or transmitted in any form or by any means, electronic, mechanical, photocopying, recording or otherwise, without the prior permission of the author. Although every precaution has been taken to verify the accuracy of the information contained herein, the publisher assume no responsibility for any errors or omissions. No liability is assumed for damages that may result from the use of information contained within.

BlueRose Publishers takes no responsibility for any damages, losses, or liabilities that may arise from the use or misuse of the information, products, or services provided in this publication.

For permissions requests or inquiries regarding this publication, please contact:

BLUEROSE PUBLISHERS
www.BlueRoseONE.com
info@bluerosepublishers.com
+91 8882 898 898
+4407342408967

ISBN: 978-93-5668-633-5

Cover design: Tahira
Typesetting: Tanya Raj Upadhyay

First Edition: February 2024

ACKNOWLEDGEMENT

I would like to thank my family, friends, near and dear ones without whom this book would not have been possible. Thank you papa(Mr. Kanti Kumar), didi (Ms. Ritika Arora)Soham(my cherubic nephew and Mrs Seema Bawa for being both, the best critics and the best support at the same time. Apart from this, I thank the myriad sources of information and knowledge which have been food for thought. Also, my take on life and my experiences I have had.

A big THANK YOU to Blue Rose publications too.

Above all, it's the grace of the Almighty and some divine intervention at work. I very strongly believe that I am just an instrument in the hands of the Divine. I have poured my mind, heart and soul so that you can see "THE RAINBOW".

Hope you enjoy it!!

Deepika Arora

FOREWARD

The seed of this book was sown during the First wave of Covid-19 at the time of lockdown. Out of all the poems some are worldly wise and some are for amusement and just for fun!! Now, it is up to the reader to figure out which one is which.

Basically, it will appeal to people from all walks of life. This book is an outcome of creative satisfaction I get and my love for playing with words...

TABLE OF CONTENTS

A SLICE OF LIFE!!!!..1

A TRIBUTE TO THE COVID-19 WARRIORS................2

A WAKE UP CALL FOR YOU ALL!!!!................................3

ACCOMPANISHING THE IMPOSSIBLE....................4

AN ODE TO THE FREE SPIRIT OF COMMON MAN..5

ATTITUDE OF GRATITUDE 6

BE A DIE HARD OPTIMIST...7

BOOZE !!BOOZE!! BOOZE!! 8

CHANGE IS THE ONLY CONSTANT................................9

RAINS IN SUMMER..10

SUMMER SUMMER YOU ARE HERE AGAIN 11

EMOTIONS AND SPORADIC FAILURE IS OK.........12

EVERYTHING HAPPENS FOR A REASON!!! 13

FAMILY LOVE 14

FATHERS AND DAUGHTERS 15

FATHERS ARE GOD SENT 16

THE ONLY FEAR TO FEAR IS FEAR 17

FINDING HAPPINESS AND BEYOND..........................18

FOR A NEAR AND DEAR ONE WITH WHOM I HAVE LOST TOUCH..19

- FORTUNE FAVOURS THE BRAVE 20
- GANDHI JAYANTI 21
- HAIL INDIAN ARMY!!!! 22
- HAPPINESS 23
- RAKSHA BANDHAN AND FAMILY BONDS 24
- HOW TO MAKE A COMEBACK AND RE-GAIN YOUR SELF 25
- I WISH I WERE A BIRD 26
- INDIA --THE WONDERFUL COUNTRY 27
- INFIDELITY 28
- IT IS WANDERLUST… 29
- KEEP SHINING 30
- KINDNESS AND ITS RIPPLE EFFECT… 31
- LIFE IS A HUSH HUSH AFFAIR… 32
- LIFE IS LIKE A BUTTERFLY, ... 33
- LIFE 34
- LISTEN TO THE NATURE 35
- ATTITUDE OF GRATITUDE SAYS IT ALL 36
- LIVE LIFE!LIVE LIFE! LIVE LIFE!!! 37
- LOVE LOVE LOVE 38
- MARRIAGE … 39
- MEDITATION AND YOGA 40
- NOTE TO MY MOTHER 41
- MONDAY MORNING BLUES … 42

MY HOSPITAL VISIT	43
NOTES AMID THE COVID-19 CHAOS…	44
WHAT SHOULD RETIREMENT BE??	45
SAVE MOTHER EARTH	46
SEE THE SUNNIER SIDE OF LIFE	48
SIBLINGS…	49
RISK AND SPECULATION	50
SUICIDE	51
TEACHER	53
THE BEAUTIFUL STORY OF WINTER AND SPRING	54
THE BEST IS YET TO COME!!!	55
THE COLOR RED!!!	56
THE COLOUR BLUE…	57
THE DIVINE LOVES YOU INDEED !!	58
THE EMPTY NEST SYNDROME!!!	59
THE PURSUIT OF HAPPINESS	60
THE TALE OF GROWTH AND PAIN.	61
THIS INDEPENDENCE DAY!!!	62
THIS TOO SHALL PASS…	63
THE WEEK AHEAD…	64
THIS VALENTINE'S DAY…..!!!!!!	65
TO DEAR PROCRASTINATION WITH LOVE…. SARCASM REDEFINED	66

UNCERTAINTY OF LIFE	68
VISIT TO HIGH COURT!!!	69
WOES OF A TAX PAYER....	70
WOMAN	71
WORDS !! WORDS!!WORDS!!!	72
YIPPEEE!!!	73
IT'S NOT ALL OVER YET!!!!	74

A SLICE OF LIFE!!!!

Life is a mystery, Oh Yes !!! It is a mystery….

Forget the stingy past,

It is history.

Open your eyes to the bright sunshine of today,

And keep positivity in the foray.

Be close to nature,

You will find goodness in every creature.

God has sent you on Earth for a reason,

Enjoy life and its every season.

Come what may, the show must go on….

Sometimes even though you have to be brave enough, have a smile to put on.

Fortune favors the brave,

And we should be positive, happy and virtuous till we hit the grave.

Life of youth is full of thrill and adventure,

Laugh and grin even if you have to put on dentures.

With lots of love and hope….A slice of life!!!!!

A TRIBUTE TO THE COVID-19 WARRIORS

Docs and nurses are the real life messengers of God,

Even without PPE many of these brave hearts are fighting the Covid-19 war.

Cops are on stringent duty mode,

Hats off to their dedication and support!!!

Electricity department has accepted the challenge,

of uninterrupted electricity 24*7.

The pen is mightier than the sword, Media personnel deserve a reward.

Kudos to the grocer, pharmacist and milkman,

Who beaver through curfews and lockdowns to reach the common man.

Videos of sweepers being honoured have flooded the net,

Humanity within us has passed the test.

Bank employees are doing a great job,

Their solidarity is something no one can rob.

These real life heroes are composed of mettle and grit,

And their undying optimism knows not how to quit.

Let's show solidarity and abide by the laws,

Love each other and ignore the flaws.

Salute and a big thank you to the Covid-19 warriors and the undying spirit of the common

man!!!!!

A WAKE UP CALL FOR YOU ALL!!!!

Were you born to eat, sleep, drink, make merry, pay bills and vanish from earth one

day???

Plan life, watch each day unfold into a new possibility to learn something new.

Do something different.

An aimless life is like a rudderless ship,

it doesn't know where it is going.

Someone truly said, comfort zone is a beautiful place,

but nothing worthwhile grows there.

We are on Earth to contribute in making positive changes;
Leave a beautiful legacy behind.

So, wake up my friend!!! Life is calling!!!!

ACCOMPANISHING THE IMPOSSIBLE...

Honor thy God gifted talent,
Do not let it go latent.
Only hard work won't suffice,
Smart work is the need of hour.
Make Big, Hairy, Audacious Goals(B-HAGS)
Along with playing different relationship roles.
Pragmatic view of life sometimes murders innovation,
So, at times, let your imagination soar high and be called crazy.
Remember, pioneers like Wright brothers were called mad when they talked about humans flying in the air.
So, in the game of life God is the referee and you are the player.
Remember Karma says,
As you sow, so shall you reap,
Give your best during the day and enjoy deep night sleep.

AN ODE TO THE FREE SPIRIT OF COMMON MAN...

Sometimes life may be messy,
And excessive work may make you dizzy.
Then remember one thing, pop up back like a spring..
And live life like a king.
Lady luck smiles at those who accept the thorns along with rose.
It is true that we get life only once
So celebrate each moment if you get the chance.

ATTITUDE OF GRATITUDE ....

To live well,
I must tell,
Gratitude is the way,
To keep unhappiness at bay.

No matter whatever your situation is,
Practice gratitude everyday and never give it a miss.
There is some Supreme Power,
Which is million times more intelligent than we are.
Rest assured you will be taken care of,
And distance off from people who react you with a scoff.
Find happiness in all seasons,
For small and big reasons.
In a life span of not more than a century,
We can learn to coexist like the floras and faunas of a wild life sanctuary.
May peace be with the human race,
And let's bask in the Almighty's grace.

BE A DIE HARD OPTIMIST....

Hope hope hope
A four lettered word,
But without which human life is nothing.
Because hope is the only dope.
And don't magnify problems with a microscope.
With hope life blooms like a beautiful rose,
And for which motivation is the daily dose.
Hope sustains life,
And gives strength to drive,
Through a crowded area.
And hope of flying high which led to invention of aeroplane.
It's hope which led Columbus to discover America, and Vasco da Gama to discover India.
It's hope which inspired ISRO to launch Chandrayan.
In fact, all the world's famous discoveries and inventions are triggered by the catalyst called hope.
Umeed par duniya kayam hai,
Yeh mann ke liye vyaayaam hai.
Isse dil-o-dimaag tandrust rehta hai,
Aur yakeen maano har khush dil yahi kehta hai,
Jab tak swaas, tab tak aas

BOOZE !!BOOZE!! BOOZE!!

Don't consume booze,

For it will blow your mind's fuse,

And leave you confuse(d),

By creating chemical imbalance in your body,

And make you appear shoddy.

Leave the addiction of booze and drugs,

Else your fortunes will go to the rugs.

These addictions are detrimental for the addict as well as the family.

And lead them to tragedy.

CHANGE IS THE ONLY CONSTANT

Sometimes heavy rains, sometimes unbearable scorching heat of the Sun....

The reason is Green House Effect and Global Warming, which is known to everyone.

The glaciers melting and the islands slowly dipping in the oceans,

Is this the beginning of an end???

Although commercialization of Solar and Wind energy has started a new trend.

Due to nature calamities so much destruction of lives and material,

This destruction doesn't differentiate whether you are a common man or an imperial.

So, let's be grateful for waking up to a new day today,

Life is fragile and many times unpredictable.

And with love for humanity,

Let's make it more liveable.

RAINS IN SUMMER....

Come Rain rain rain!!!
Take away parched Earth's pain.
With the much awaited downpour,
The dark clouds roar.
The hailstorm has a view which is a spectacular one,
And the white sheet of hails is rejoiced by everyone.
The cool breeze is so relaxing,
It's made our day chillaxing.
The roads bathed in the rain look so clean and clear,

Many want to go on a long drive with some chilled beer.
The white clouds have been shadowed with dark rainy ones,
The game between dark and white clouds tossing each other,
Is a view everyone would likes to view and bother.
Thank You Almighty for the rains today,
It's also nature' heyday.

SUMMER SUMMER YOU ARE HERE AGAIN

Hey Summer!!! Here u come,

With Mango, Watermelon and Litchi among the fruit delicacies,

Sitting under trees with cool breeze increases the farmers' efficiency.

Cold Coffee, Lemonade, fruit juices and squashes are in the survival module,

The summer camps make the schedule of kids" jam-packed."

Swimming is the ultimate refuge for the sun rays drenched body and scorching heat .

Sporadic rainfall gives temporary relief to the summer heat,

Dear Almighty bless us all!!!

EMOTIONS AND SPORADIC FAILURE IS OK...

It's ok to fall sometimes,

To feel low sometimes.

To cry and feel sad,

For this is what makes us human and differentiates us from robots.

Life becomes easy when one's EQ(emotional Quotient) is good,

For today IQ without EQ is a husband without wife and vice-versa.

SQ (spiritual quotient)is another newbie today,

For it sorts out mental health issues n keeps psychosomatic illnesses at bay.

So, let's be positive n crib less and make everyday a beautiful day.

EVERYTHING HAPPENS FOR A REASON!!!

Yes, everything happens for a reason,
There are happiness and pain in every season.
Life is beautiful if one sees beyond,
Forgive and forget if someone has done you wrong.
To live well is the greatest revenge,
Don't fall into the negativity trench.

Yes!! everything happens for a reason....
Good things happen to those who believe, pouring your heart in prayers can give you relief and lessen the grief.

Yes!! everything happens for a reason...
Trust God's MASTER PLAN,
He will take care of your friends and clan.

Yes!! everything happens for a reason!!
Like a river let life take its course,
You will see miracles you have never seen before,
Together we can achieve more...
Yes!! everything happens for a reason..

FAMILY LOVE

O!! What is life sans family?

It's room without roof,

A ship without sail,

A lonely peak standing tall.

A wielded tree without flowers.

A desert without oasis.

Life is so incomplete without family love.

For those who have it, it is a blessing from above.

Rejoice it, live it and value it because life is a onetime affair.

FATHERS AND DAUGHTERS

Father is a daughters' first hero,
Without his love and care, her happiness is almost zero
Father and daughter share a special bond,
He is like a magic wand.
Daughter is Papa's princess,
And even a small gift from him is priceless.
A daughter is like papa ki pari,
When he is there she has nothing to worry.
None can replace a dad's selfless love,
In his priority list, he treats her above (everything)

FATHERS ARE GOD SENT

Fathers are God 's unique gifts

They bind the family when between it there are drifts.

Tirelessly they fend for the family,

They are the family' safety net and the Canopy,

Which ensure safety n comfort.

Blessed are those who have doting fathers,

They protect when no one bothers.

Life is a smooth ride when dads are there,

They spread love, care, happiness, humour and warmth everywhere.

They are the guiding light in the dark phases of life,

They inculcate the fight back spirit and teach us how to strife.

Be it teaching us academic or life's lessons,

Their wisdom is the life's protocol handbook for all seasons.

THE ONLY FEAR TO FEAR IS FEAR

Fear fear fear...why this fear,
When God is there my dear.
Sometimes the Supreme power tests our faith,
By giving challenges so that we may become great.
Life may be topsy turvy and a roller coaster ride,
So, be humble and leave the pride.
Don't let this human life go waste,
Experience it's each season and it's every taste.
Remember everything happens for our own good,
So cheer up and leave the melancholy mood.
Never let fear overcome your vision,
For it will blur the vision….
The more fearless you become,
The lesser you will be disturbed by life's humdrum.

FINDING HAPPINESS AND BEYOND...

Finding happiness in the mundane is tricky,

It is somewhat crikey.

While making friends be a little picky.

Life is what you make it,

Don't be adamant, flexibility in attitude will make it.

Everyone goes through a rough patch,

How to be happy is the catch.

Good deeds are like debit card,

You pay now and enjoy later,

Bad deeds are like credit card,

You enjoy now and pay later,

So, be vigilant regarding what you do,

This will make the journey of life liveable too.

FOR A NEAR AND DEAR ONE WITH WHOM I HAVE LOST TOUCH.

Dear one, where r u?
Please give me some cue.
I like talking to you,
You seem so humble,
When you are near I will never tumble.
Knowing you is an honour,
Please reply soon,
You are like the full moon
With Soft light, and calm attitude.
I thank Almighty with gratitude,
that I came to know u,
You are pure and shine like morning dew.
Please reply soon,
Don't disappear in the clouds like the moon.

FORTUNE FAVOURS THE BRAVE

Fortune favours the brave....

Lady luck smiles at those

who accept the thorns along with rose.

It's better to burn out than to fade away,

Be optimistic, if you are struggling, God will clear your way.

Bravery is definitely an asset,

As it tends to bring out your best.

A big smile and a happy face can uplift you from melancholy,

It helps to peacefully

rectify your folly

When life throws lemons at you,

Make lemonade with it.

For happiness and success, bravery and confidence are the toolkit

Keep rocking, keep moving,

Keep doing your bit

Good fortune will definitely give you something which will fit (in)

O Yes!!!fortune favours the brave.

GANDHI JAYANTI....

Here comes the birthday of our beloved Father of the nation,
For whom to see independent India was a passion.
Bapu we miss you today,
But you must be happy in the heaven above to see India making her way.
Swadeshi, Make- in- India and Swatch Bharat were your dreams,
That have been fulfilled by PM Modi and his team.
You are an inspiration to one and all,
Hope we Indians prevent our international standing from having a fall.
Your compassion for the downtrodden is unmatched,
Self reliance is the golden egg that has hatched .
Today India is a young nation,
And our India is God's wonderful creation.
Hail Father of the Nation!!!
Jai Hind!!!

HAIL INDIAN ARMY!!!!

Indian Army rocks!!! They work round the clock.

A big salute to the soldiers braving the chilly winds in Leh & Ladakh,

Far away from their kith and kin.

Living lives in solitude,

On lonely tops of rocks and hills.

Sometimes on day and sometime on night duty.

Their duty is hard,

In comparison to them we have cushy jobs.

Putting their lives in danger,

They serve the nation.

For them its' less of a duty, more of a passion.

Lets' pray for our jawaans and their families,

For they are the reason we are secure,

happy and enjoy sound sleep.

JAI HIND!!!!

HAPPINESS ..

True and long lasting Happiness is found when we go inward and within,
Find joy in small and petty moments of life and you will cut many birthday cakes with knife (as true happiness increases the life span)
It is said that God loves fun,
So he plays with us and brings challenges when you expect none.
The key is to give your best and be prepared for the worst,
Read your holy scriptures and don't let them gather dust.
Don't worry be happy,
Make Ur conversations upmarket and peppy.
Keep moving, keep working and rekindle hope,
When in stress,
Meditation can be the ultimate dope.
Life is beautiful when friends become family and family becomes friends,
Dress up smartly and trailblaze new trends.
Life may sometimes be meandering like a river,
But faith on God should not waver.
Kindness and happiness go hand in hand,
Where one is present the other one is bound to follow,
Without them, life becomes sunken and hollow.
Keep shining keep up the chirpiness alive,
Be a receptor of only good vibe.
Live love and have fun,
To keep fit have a good run.

RAKSHA BANDHAN AND FAMILY BONDS

Happy Raksha Bandhan to all the beautiful people reading this,

May this day fill you with bliss!!!

Brother sister bond is so beautiful,

It's a reminder for both bro and sis to be dutiful,

Sister is like the pink rose

And brother is the fragrance which the Amighty chose

To complete and protect it.

Parents are the thorns which protect the flower,

They are proof of Almighty's power.

When in trouble,

Surrender n pray to the Almighty...He will burst the misery bubble.

Today may

Your happiness get double...

HOW TO MAKE A COMEBACK AND RE-GAIN YOUR SELF

Everybody goes through turbulence,
Some less some more,
Let there be light,
And bring tranquility with all your might .
Don't loose heart,
And give life a new start.
Everyday is a new opportunity to re-write your destiny,
Live life the way you want but at times do scrutiny,
As to what's your destination and where are you headed,
What are your debit Karma and what are your credit.
Let there be a balance between fun, frolic and sincerity.

A few words for everyone making a comeback in life....

I WISH I WERE A BIRD

Fly high in the sky.

Binging on fruits and vegetables in orchards and fields.

Watching Earth from a height,

And using my wings with all my might.

Watching sunrise and sunset from a coastline,

Meeting my fellow migratory birds on the way back home.

Maybe as a Woodpecker,

Drilling trees or as Taylor bird weaving my nest,

Cuddling with my family and taking rest.

Or maybe a Kingfisher,

Proudly showing my colorful wings,

Or a Peacock dancing in the rain,

Or simply a sparrow chirping in vain but never in pain.

INDIA --THE WONDERFUL COUNTRY

From Kashmir to Kanyakumari,
Languages change from Dogri, Tamil to Bihari.
The Aravali hills/mountains stand tall,
And we love the soothing Karnataka's Jog falls.
The lush green fields dance to the music of wind in Punjab.
Gujarat has folklores of the Nawab.
The lions roar with pride in the Gir forest,
In Ranthambore wildlife sanctuary flora and fauna peacefully take rest .
All the forts and fortresses of Rajasthan sing the valor tales of the Rajas and Maharajas.

All in the seven sisters reflect the serene beauty of nature.
In UP, a dip in the holy river Ganga gives deep bliss and purifies the devotees.
The Taj Mahal, the epitome of true love,
And one of the seven wonders of the world,
Seems so perfect as if dropped from the Heavens above.

The sea shores of coastal areas and oceans so wide,
Love blooms in the oceans' every tide.
The mountains and hill stations bathe in the divine snow and snow covered peaks
bask in the beautiful Sun...
Kudos to the incredible India!!!

INFIDELITY....

Infidelity makes a person lose his credibility.

It breaks the trust,

And collapses the sacred communion of marriage to dust.

Fidelity is worth the pain,

Life tests our faith and abiding to spouse in sun and rain.

Marriage is a journey of two souls,

After it, both have to play many different roles.

The lady is sister, daughter, lover, wife

And the gentleman is brother, son, lover, husband.

So, pick your spouse with care,

So that fights are rare.

IT IS WANDERLUST...

O yes it is indeed wanderlust!!

Nobody can inhibit my wanderlust for ideas,
It's what keeps me ticking,
And help me rekindle the flame of zest and enthusiasm from flickering .
Life of a wanderlust is brimming up with various colours; opportunities for growth,
both personal and professional,
All you need is intellect, intuition and being rational.
Wanderlust is for free spirited souls,
Who know not insecurity and lethargy,
It's common for a bohemian heart and soul.
O yes!! Indeed it's wanderlust which fills the heart with excitement and keeps
boredom at bay.
It's a testimony of the fact that change is the only constant,
And makes love for change abundant.
O yes !! It's indeed wanderlust,
It has put monotony to dust,
Because to rest is to rust.
Kudos to the bohemian spirit!!!!

KEEP SHINING ....

Don't keep basking in yesterday's glory,
The day is gone and it's an old story.
Achieve something every day,
This will keep self doubt at bay.
An aimless life is a total waste,
Keep your heart and head clean and chaste.
Life is short and so much to achieve,
Have the confidence and the belief.
Believe me when you harness your focus,
It will help keep life away from mayhem and ruckus.
Life's battles are always won by those who believe,
Just surrender to the Supreme, it will give you relief.

KINDNESS AND ITS RIPPLE EFFECT...

Being kind is a virtue and an asset,
When you practice it, you won't regret.
Life becomes beautiful for its doer and the receiver,
It prevents one from unhappiness and self centeredness.

As the joy is more in giving than receiving,
Donation, philanthropy, kindness and good karmas go hand in hand,
They are the ultimate magic wand.
Happiness derived out of kindness is ultimate,
It brings trust in humanity which non can replicate.
Be kind to yourself too…Let life take its course, find a way or make one.
Be kind to self and recognise you are second to none.
Slowly and steadily, take one step at a time.
Let each day be a new chapter of your life.
Let the mystery of life unfold...
Rejoice it, live it and surrender to the supreme when required.
Just pray that you get enough prudence of when to hold on when to surrender.

LIFE IS A HUSH HUSH AFFAIR…..

LIFE is short,
So much is yet to be done.
To keep fit go for a run,
Never give up unless your work is done.
Enjoy and experience every colour of life,
Whether you are someone's husband or wife.
Life is beautiful if one sees beyond,
For miracles to happen,
Prayer is the magic wand.
Keep focused, stay calm and God will do the rest,
He will help you pass life's every test.
Eat and drink healthy, and meditate, this will keep away problems and not
exaggerate.
Enjoy the cocktail of life,
Experience the colours of the rainbow of life…
Keep moving, keep enjoying what God has bestowed upon you,
You will shine like the morning dew……

LIFE IS LIKE A BUTTERFLY,

It's fragile, it's beautiful,
It's unpredictable.
It comes in many colours and designs,
And searches for happiness here and there,
Like a butterfly hops from flower to flower in search of nectar.
It's difficult to catch,
And its unique, has no match.
Just like a caterpillar goes through extreme pain to transform into a beautiful
butterfly,
Same is life, through challenges, it finally teaches us how to fly under the blue sky.

LIFE

Life is tough, sometimes it plays bluff.

May God bless all of us,

Join the bandwagon of happiness and don't miss the bus.

Don't be a procrastinator,

Do stuff which makes you the best version of the Creator.

Don't panic in tough situations,

Follow your heart and listen to your passion.

It's true we live only once,

So, enjoy life whenever you get the chance.

(L)ove for humanity

(I)nterest in goodness

(F)aith in the Supreme power

(E)mpathy for others

This is what makes LIFE..,

Make it big...

LISTEN TO THE NATURE....

Listen to the cuckoo singing,
It keeps the happiness ringing.
The waterfall sings and dances on the stones,
It enlivens the heart which mourns.
Red rose smells like Heaven,
And as relaxing as visiting a tavern.
The gentle breeze is so soothing,
It helps lift up mood when u feel like brooding.
The windy days add fervour to life,
It helps you sooth from everyday strife.
Wet soil smells ecstatic,
It brings true joy which is otherwise so erratic.
Rain wipes away all the pain,
And washes it down the drain.
The Sunflower smiles and dances so happily at the Sun,
It inspires everyone.
The dew drops shine so bright on the grass,
That it's view lets sadness definitely pass....
O Yes!!!! Listen to the nature

ATTITUDE OF GRATITUDE SAYS IT ALL...

Thank the Almighty that you woke up today,
Another beautiful day,
You being the CEO of your life,
Cut away shackles with the positivity knife.
Don't give the steering of your life in someone else's hand.
Prayer and gratitude are the ultimate magic wand.
Thank the universe for all the good things you have.
So many of our less fortunate brethren don't have them.
When life is going downhill,
Don't blame God for a thing gone wrong; life gets full circle and its karma that boomerangs.

LIVE LIFE!LIVE LIFE! LIVE LIFE!!!

Don't worry, be happy..
Have Cappuccino if not Frappé
Shoo away the worry
Else it'll make the vision blurry.
To take up life's challenges
You'll have to exercise your phalanges.
Wake up!life is calling
Faith in Supreme and self will prevent you from falling.
With a head held high
Face life and touch the sky.
Talk less and listen more
But prevent yourself from becoming a bore.
Learn to let go,
And you will definitely grow.
Shed away the emotional baggage
It may not be easy, take it as a challenge.
A smiling face and a positive mindset
Will help you cope up when you are upset.
Dream big and achieve more
Live your life a folklore.

LOVE LOVE LOVE

Love is the best emotion of all,
As it acts as a protective wall.. .
It protects one from emotional turmoil,
As it acts as a foil
Against negativity and insecurity.
It may be eros, storge, philia or agape,
And helps keep up life in shape.
Life goes for a toss when love is missing,
Happiness is hacked as negativity goes phishing.
Love brings bliss and ecstasy in life for
dreamers who tie the knot to be husband and wife.
The family love is irreplaceable….
I just pray none has to strive much to bring it in life…..

Har kisi ko nahi milta yahan pyar zindagi mein, khush naseeb hai woh jinko hai mili yeh bahaar
zindagi mein
------With wishes for a happy n love filled life for all.

MARRIAGE .....

Marriage is a communion of two souls.
Start this journey with a red rose.
There are ups and there are downs,
Don't exaggerate negativity with frowns.
When Life throws lemons at you,
Make lemonade out of it.
For saving your relationship do your bit.
Marriage is a roller coaster ride,
Every girl remembers the day she becomes the bride.
With time, let the relationship mature,
Just like a bud ripens into a rose.
Ignore the flaws and focus on strengths,
Let love grow deep and dense.

MEDITATION AND YOGA

Meditation and yoga are the new cool,
They are now taught even in school.
The meditative state of mind is sheer bliss,
It's more refreshing than lemonade with fizz.
The blessings of SPIRITUAL MASTER are must,
They can elevate ones' state of mind to higher realms from dust.
Guru Bina gati nahi,
Dhyan Bina sumati nahi.
The more polished meditator you become,
The less affected you will be from life's humdrum.
The closer you are to the MASTER,
Your spiritual side grows faster.

NOTE TO MY MOTHER

MISS U MAA...
Mumma I miss you
Moms like you are very few.
Wish you were here,
To rejoice my success my dear.
Life seems a roller coaster ride,
You are my first love and my pride.
You are my inspiration,
Life without you is asphyxiation.
You taught me resilience,
And the importance of silence.
It is said God could not be everywhere so he created mothers,
Without you nobody much bothers.
Dear God, please send my mother back,

I know this wish will make me appear a crack
I am sure our souls will meet again,
Needless to say I am in pain.
My eyes are full of tears,
I still miss you after so many years.

Love u miss u mumma....

MONDAY MORNING BLUES ...

Monday morning blues...come in different hues!!
Some have after party hangovers,
Some have nostalgia of holidays spent well.
Most kids go to school with a heavy heart,
Saturday and Sunday play a vital part,
They help maintain a work- life balance,
And help stop stress from evoking menace.
However, there is no rest for women, be it working or homemakers,
On weekends most of them turn into chefs and bakers.
Come Friday and the feeling of ecstasy seeps in,
Life starts seeming rosy and beautiful,
But Mondays make us dutiful..

MY HOSPITAL VISIT...

Went to a govt. hospital today
Don't know what to say!!!
Saw depressed and unhappy souls rushing to emergency ward.
Seeing blood and medicines was definitely not on my card.
The brave heart nurses and docs working day and night,
Giving hope to people with all their might.
It is true that docs are Gods in disguise,
They are intelligent and wise.
Health care workers have to put in emotional labor
In order to curb their patients' hope from waver.
Covid or no Covid, they are always frontline warriors
Against diseases from all sort of carriers!!!!
A BIG SALUTE to the spirit of a health care professional!!!

NOTES AMID THE COVID-19 CHAOS...

With the lockdown,

Life has slowed down.

Nature has pressed the pause and reset buttons,

Non veggies are desperate for their chicken and muttons.

Air flights have been cancelled,

Busy life been seriously hampered.

Ozone layer is on repair mode

As there are almost no vehicles on the road.

Trains converted into isolation centers,

Unemployed youth looking for mentors.

The skyline is crystal clear,

Suddenly the birds have nothing to fear.

As they say"every dark cloud has a silver lining"

All family members at home are together dining.

Inspite of social distancing emotionally family and friends are closer now,

The pride of human beings as being the most powerful has taken a bow.

Amid curfews, lockdowns and crisis,

One thing is for sure, we will definitely find a covid19 cure.

After the chaos is over, life will be never the same before,

And for the coming generations covid19 in 2020 will be a folklore.

WHAT SHOULD RETIREMENT BE??

R(ESTLESS for doing some productive work)
E(NTHUSIASTIC for life)
T(HIRST for knowledge)
I(NQUISITIVE nature)
R(EKINDLE faith)
E(AGERNESS to learn)

SO....RETIRE as above

SAVE MOTHER EARTH

Save mother Earth O dear save mother Earth!!
Mother Earth is our nurturer,
It's water is it's blood,
Deforestation causes flood.
She is in pain,
Humans have harmed her so much for personal gain.

Save mother Earth O Save mother Earth
Global warming has harmed her so much,
Glaciers are melting and it's a total glitch.

Save mother Earth O Save mother Earth
She is crying loud and is in discomfort,
Aforestation can sooth her and give her comfort.
Floods and cyclones keep us reminding
time and again,
Don't harm her further and relieve her pain.
The floras and faunas have been damaged to such an extent,
I doubt we survive it beyond a certain extend.

It's time to be beware before the game is over,
Don't let her die with deforestation, global warming and Green House Effect which
can cause her incurable fever.

The ball is in our court,
Let's play the game well.
Yes!!! Indeed let's save mother Earth

SEE THE SUNNIER SIDE OF LIFE

See the sunnier side of life,
For that you may even have to strive.
Realise and believe you deserve the best,
For that u may even have to pass the Almighty's test.
Delve deep within,
And let wisdom seep in.
Let there be light,
And fight darkness with all your might.
Life is beautiful if one sees beyond,
Stop living the life of a frog in the pond.
Realise how blessed you are to be born as human being,
Have faith, the Supreme will take care of your well being.

SIBLINGS....

Blessed are those who have siblings,
None can replace the sibling love,
They are gifts from the Heavens above.
They fight, they care and they are the guiding light,
They make a dull life shine bright.
They keep secrets both good and bad,
And help cheer up when you are sad.
It's true blood is thicker than water,
Elder siblings will take care of you like their son and daughter.
Three cheers to the SIBLINGS LOVE...whose heart is tender and pure as the dove

RISK AND SPECULATION ....

Speculation...
Speculation speculation
Speculation!!!
Life is all about speculation,
And it's all about risk.
To eat is to speculate for food poisoning,
To drive is to risk for accident.
One needs to be brave enough
Else life will play bluff.
Bulls and bears may make your life a roller coaster ride.
So, take calculated risk in your stride.
To rest is to rust,
So, take the plunge and dive deep within.
Adventure of life is worth taking risk,
And speculation depends upon prediction,
Intuition and becoming brisk.
Keep moving, keep learning and keep speculating sensibly.

SUICIDE

Suicide is not the right choice my dear,
If you are going through a rough patch, learn to bear.
Life is topsy turvy for everyone,
For some more or some less,
Pray to God and he will bless!!

Don't have a feeble heart,
To get the right mindset is an art.
Don't blow your mind over petty things,
As everyone is going through a gruel,
Sometimes life may appear cruel.

For problems are inevitable,
But to go through problems is vital.
Some have no job so they are sad,
And some find their job tough so they are mad.
Some are searching for the right spouse and are desperate,
Others have a spouse but they are exasperate.

Some are students and disheartened about their grades,
So, everybody faces tough situations and their many shades,
All I wanna say is,
get up and get going,

So that you get the fruits of the positive approach that you are sowing (in your head)

Let your soul connect with the master soul,

And you will understand your purpose in life as a whole...

TEACHER

Every little creature is a teacher.

You have to be prudent enough to be a student.

The ant teaches industry,

The fragrance of rose teaches chemistry.

The lion teaches self confidence,

The tiger, teaches to be a fighter.

The nightingale, to be sweet come what may.

The elephant, to be thick skinned.

The water, to be adjustable but still persistent enough to make way through rocks.

The Sun, to shine even if you are alone.

The Moon to be beautiful inspite of craters, and celebrate its beauty in imperfection itself.

So, hang on dearies!!! Celebrate Teacher's day because learning should never stop come what may!!!!

THE BEAUTIFUL STORY OF WINTER AND SPRING

IT's Winter..

The winters are here again,

Some say they are gloomy,

For some they are romantic.

I think it's a blend of both.

Because trees become stunted and there is no growth.

And winters make you enjoy hot hot broth and coffee with froth.

Besan laddu, pinni and gajar ka halwa

Along with kesar milk is sheer jalwaa.

Well packed in winter clothes,

We resemble stuffed toys and teady bears,

Some enjoy winters with chilled beer.

Christmas, New year and Lohri

Fun with family and friends,

They are the ones who are our strengths.

As with them our nature blends.

As Spring is round the corner,

Flowers will bloom as we will celebrate Basant Panchami,

Colors, kites and high pitched music will be there in North India...

So...Winters come and winters go,

With full pomp and show...

THE BEST IS YET TO COME!!!

The best is yet to come,

So many challenges are yet to Overcome.

Set Dreams, ambitions and lofty idols

With a head held high and confidence face all your rivals.

O yes!! The best is yet to come....

Optimism, confidence, hope and love

Are all blessings from the heavens above.

There is this one life to live, love and achieve,

Have profound faith in your believe.

Keep moving, keep achieving and never loose hope

Even if life's going down the slope.

THE COLOR RED!!!

Red --- the color of rose and also of human blood.

Watermelon, Tomato and Zomato have the same thing in common,

They all brag of the color red.

The danger sign of 440Volts where skull and crossed bones as the symbol of danger also adorned by

the color red .

The color of red hot fire of hell to the color of passion is indeed RED.

It's the color of sindhoor on the forehead of Indian bride.

So, without red you are dead….

THE COLOUR BLUE...

Blue is the affirmation that the nature is with you.
It is the hue of the vast sky,
The color of infinite ocean and sea,
And the hue of lord Krishna and Shiva,
It reminds of the omnipresence of the Supreme,
And the infinite realm of God.
It helps strength the believe that u can fight odds,
But blue shouldn't be the hue of Monday morning blues,
For that one has to find a work one is passionate about,
And then mind will be happy without any doubt.
So... without blue, who are you??

THE DIVINE LOVES YOU INDEED !!

The divine loves you…,

The sky loves you; keeping you warm through Sun, provides you water through rain.

The Earth loves you, it holds you through gravity,

It provides trees; through which you get air to breathe and food to eat.

It provides spectacular views of snowfall during winters,

And mangoes and watermelons to relish in summers.

Indeed the divine love is all miracles; how could otherwise roses smell so ecstatic,

And dolphins be so human friendly; How could migratory birds remember their homes to go back.

How could Eagle fly above the clouds,

How could a young one by born!!!

In a nutshell, never crib, because come what may, the divine beholds you,

This is the magnanimity and the endless love of the divine!!!

THE EMPTY NEST SYNDROME!!!

An empty nest syndrome is a stark reality of Indian Diaspora.

Elderly parents waiting for their now grown up kids,

And parents selling their empty homes in bids.

Old age homes are becoming the new normals of NRI fraternity,

NRI kids find it difficult to keep up promises of being with their parents till eternity.

Parent- child relationship is a pious relation,

Grandchildren love to visit their grandpa and grandma during their vacation.

Money rules the roost in most youngsters ' life,

Hence they settle in far off lands and strive.

Gone are the days of joint families,

Nuclear ones are in vogue,

And old age homes are the prologue.

The once busy households are now drenched in spells of loneliness,

Proud parents of NRI kids sink into gloomy and depressive phases,

With fine wrinkles on their faces.

THE PURSUIT OF HAPPINESS.....

Some running after tangible acquisition,
Some after intangible ones.
Life has become a struggle for luxuries,
For achieving this, he has to undergo some atrocities.
Rolls Royce, BMW or Merc,
Running after them can make you go beserk.
In the wake of glamour,
Simplicity has taken a beating,
And to flaunt material possessions,
People can even resort to cheating.
Tommy, Gucci, Versace, Prada or Jimmy Choo
People going mad that they could have it too.
But the bottom line is,
Are you innately happy or just living in illusionary happiness.
It's a million dollar answer which can remove life's crankiness..

THE TALE OF GROWTH AND PAIN.

Growth and pain go hand in hand.

Only after pain growth is possible,

A caterpillar goes through tremendous pain while transforming into the beautiful

butterfly.

So, take it easy and don't give a sigh.

It's only under infinite pressure does coal become diamond.

And it's only after heavy rains does a rainbow appear in the sunny sky.

Remember, nature has its own sweet and fair way to bring out the best in us.

So, don't let the hope and confidence take a beating.

Remember no pain, no gain

"Ruk Jana Nahi Kahi Tu haar ke,

Kaanto pe chalke milenge saaye bhaar ke"

THIS INDEPENDENCE DAY!!!

Happy INDEPENDENCE DAY to all,
May our country never have a fall,
And may our future endeavours stand tall .
Ho ghar ghar TIRANGA,
Hum Indians se nahi ho koi behtar aur na hi koi changa.
Let's do our bit to contribute to society and nation building,
Stop the BRAIN DRAIN and refrain from sulking
That things are not favorable.
Because they can be manageable.

And make every city a SMART City...
Let's all Indians vow to combat corruption and mediocrity,
Vandey Mataram!!!
Jai Hind!!!

THIS TOO SHALL PASS....

Life may not always be hunky dory
But we can always bask in the Almighty's glory.
Stop feeling sorry for yourself...
Remember this too shall pass

Be humble and grounded like the grass.
Self pity is a psychological crime
So surrender your problems to the Supreme be it in church, temple, gurudwara or
shrine
What goes up comes down
So why the pride and why the frown?
Life is like a bubble
So by arrogance and self centeredness why invite the trouble?
Happiness is a state of mind
And everyone has to go through the grind.
The present moment is a chance to become great
So why not rejoice and celebrate?
Remember, this too shall pass
So clear the mental clutter and the crass ...
And dance to Country, Rock or Jazz

THE WEEK AHEAD....

Today is Sunday, hope it turns out to be a fun day.

Welcome new week with open arms,

May it bring serenity, novelty and calm.

So, No Monday morning blues,

Color your day with interesting hues.

Hope Tuesday turns out to be productive,

For workoholic work itself is seductive.

Wednesday not be a tryst day.

Thursday vibes bring a zing in the air.

Friday is soothing, takes away all the sulking and brooding.

Saturday is incomparably relaxing…

Anyways, life goes on and on,

And have a happy end to the weekend.

THIS VALENTINE'S DAY.....!!!!!!

Valentine's Day is almost here
Love is in the air,
Hope singles find their better half soon
And the committed people's love bloom
Time for chocolates, cards and flowers is here
Love songs are being played everywhere
Amid the warmth of evening bonfire
Champagne n brandy can enhance the love desire
Hope this valentine's Day is special and lucky for all
And everyone finds their inner call....
Love all!!!

TO DEAR PROCRASTINATION WITH LOVE....
SARCASM REDEFINED

Procrastination!! Procrastination !! Procrastination !!!

Who doesn't know you???

You are born in a family where father is disinterest and mother is negativity. Your twin is

delay, elder sister is postponement, younger sister is laziness and brother is demotivation.

Your uncle is malnutrition and aunt is undernutrition.

Procrastination!! Procrastination!!! Procrastination!!

Procrastination hits people of all ages and walks of life.

You are one of the reasons a husband fights with his wife.

Kids procrastinate studies for playtime

And toddlers do it because they dislike to mug up their dodging tables and nursery rhyme.

Procrastination !! Procrastination !! Procrastination !!

The aged who are on pills and medicines often procrastinate taking them,

And prime reason

Why an employee gets fired be it any season.

To shoo you away,

One needs consistent effort,

When you go away,

It improves a person's honour and rapport.

Procrastination !!

Procrastination!!
Procrastination !!

The day you go away from someone's life,
Is a celebration after the strife.
------- with a pinch of dark sarcasm …

UNCERTAINTY OF LIFE....

Life is uncertain,
Then why take so much of burden.
Take each day as it comes,
Cherish some time with your chums.
Tik tok tik goes the clock,
Stand firm and concrete like the rock.
Live free, live happy,
Have Capuchinno if not Frappe..
Take some time out of the rat race,
Let positivity ooze out of your face.
Never give up come what may,
Live to the fullest each and ever day.

VISIT TO HIGH COURT!!!

Today I visited the Punjab and Haryana High Court,
And saw intellectual robots,
Clad in white shirts and black coats.
Advocates talking in legal jargon,
Among all the mayhem and chaos
Of a blend of lawyers of all ages and experiences.
Men and women debating for their clientele,
In courtrooms adorned by honourable judges,
Courtrooms are like churches, where prayers are filed and petitions are heard, and
the theory of karma beholds.
Where fight for truth and principal of natural justice prevails.

WOES OF A TAX PAYER....

A tax payer!!

I am a proud tax payer,

In other words , a poverty slayer.

A common man is torn apart between the need to save and an urge to spend.

Due to no social security, he is always worried about his end(days)

Be it GST, IT or Property Tax,

One is always busy paying one after the other tax; that makes us dizzy.

The authorities never seem to have enough,

We are caught in web of taxes and it seems to play bluff.

No clear accountability and no transparency of where our hard earned money goes,

All we hear is scams and other woes!!!

WOMAN ....

A woman is a sister, daughter, lover, wife.
Cares she does and for you does she strive,
with the whole world.
Life becomes Heaven when you get the optimistic woman,
And hell if she turns out to be sarcastic and narcissist.
She is the epitome of love and sacrifice.
Growing up I have seen my granny's selfless and pure love,
She was a fairy from the Heaven's above.
Mom too was one of the most selfless ones I know,
We all miss you both I wanna tell you.
True it is, that, we get good women by good fortunes,
But wrong ones can degenerate it to ruins.

WORDS !! WORDS!!WORDS!!!

Be careful about words.....For they have the power to hurt.

And sometimes make a genuine person seem like a pervert!!!

Words can make or mar a relationship,

Be it nuptial, platonic, altruistic / plain friendship.

Words are born in mind and travel through verbal or written expression,

Right ones required to make a good impression.

Over the time playing with them has become my passion.

Imagine a world without them,

The world would be dumb, deaf or mute...Right flow of them can make

communication flow like beautiful music on a flute.....

YIPPEEE!!!

Ping pong ping,
And I wanna sing,
And shout out loud,
Aaj jeelo zaraa,
Kal ka nahi pataa

IT'S NOT ALL OVER YET!!!!

O yes !! It's not all over yet,

Keep the hope alive till you are dead.

Life may be topsy turvy and everything may appear to go wrong,

So to free yourself from negativity, visit the temple and listen to the gong,

Or maybe listen to some devotional or motivational song .

O yes!!It's not all over!!!and you are not dead!!

Have big hairy audacious goals,

Play well all the roles God has bestowed upon.

Success will come to you when you are prepared for the opportunity and respond to

His cue .

Growth is painful,

Painful still is change, but more painful is to be at the place where you don't belong.

Keep the hope alive and success will be in range.

Keep yourself upfront and exercise your skills lest they become blunt.

Dream, do and be alive from within,

Never let negativity seep in.

Indeed!!! All is not yet over and this is not the end.

www.ingramcontent.com/pod-product-compliance
Lightning Source LLC
LaVergne TN
LVHW061559070526
838199LV00077B/7105